Original title:
Architecture of Almost

Copyright © 2024 Creative Arts Management OÜ
All rights reserved.

Author: Seraphina Caldwell
ISBN HARDBACK: 978-9916-90-564-7
ISBN PAPERBACK: 978-9916-90-565-4

The Art of Breached Expectations

In shadows cast by dreams that fray,
We wander paths where choices lay.
The weight of hope, it bends the light,
Yet sparks of change ignite the night.

Through every turn, a lesson sown,
In fractures, we find seeds we've grown.
The heart expands beyond its cage,
Transforming pain into the stage.

Bastions of the Unfinished

In quiet corners, futures wait,
With echoes of an open gate.
We linger where the canvas breathes,
And paint our truth with whispered heaves.

Each story hangs, a thread unspooled,
In every risk, a vision fueled.
Beneath the doubt, a fire burns,
For in the half-made, the heart returns.

Ascending from Uncertainty

Upon the edge of weeping doubt,
We lift our eyes to stars that shout.
A step through mist, uncertain ground,
Yet in this chaos, hope is found.

With every heartbeat, whispers rise,
A melody beneath the skies.
In swirling fog, a glimpse of grace,
Each moment's sway, a soft embrace.

The Language of Signposts Unseen

In every thought, a symbol lies,
A whisper tangled in the skies.
With eyes attuned to cryptic signs,
We navigate where fate aligns.

The journey speaks in silent threads,
In paths unknown, our spirit treads.
With every choice, a map we weave,
In unseen words, we come to believe.

The Geometry of Hopes

In angles and curves, dreams take flight,
They weave through the shadows, chasing the light.
Each line a potential, each point a new start,
Mapping the realms of the hopeful heart.

On grids of ambition, we sketch our desires,
Constructing a vision that never expires.
With every intersection, we gather our schemes,
Building a future that fuels our dreams.

Tethered by Possibility

With threads of connection that weave through the air,
We dance on the edges, envisioning rare.
The ties that bind us in vibrant display,
Draw us together, come what may.

Each hope a balloon, rising with grace,
Affixed to the ground, finding its place.
A tapestry woven with colors so bright,
Tethered by possibility, destined for flight.

Misty Foundations

In the haze of uncertainty, we stand firm and tall,
Laying the stones, where shadows enthrall.
With each whispered promise, we build our domain,
A sanctuary crafted amidst joy and pain.

Foundations in mist, yet sturdy we rise,
Vision clear as the sun, piercing the skies.
Through the fog, we navigate, with courage we strive,
Misty foundations help our dreams thrive.

Echoing Aspirations

In valleys of whispers, our wishes resound,
Each echo a promise, in silence profound.
The mountains listen, as dreams intertwine,
In the symphony of hope, our spirits align.

From heights of ambition, we shout to the stars,
Unfurling our dreams, no matter how far.
Through the echoes, we journey, together, we stand,
United in aspirations, hand in hand.

Faded Visions

In the dusk, dreams slip away,
Whispers lost in shades of gray.
Memories fade, like smoke in air,
Echoes linger; we seldom care.

Once vibrant hues now dull and cold,
Stories forgotten, tales untold.
Eyes that glimmer, now dimmed and worn,
Hope retreats at each new dawn.

Paths Left Untraveled

Winding trails beneath the trees,
Silent beckon in the breeze.
Footsteps linger, tracing time,
Choices scattered, once sublime.

Bridges broken, lost in mist,
Journeys missed, the heart's sweet twist.
Promises whispered on the road,
Visions fade, dreams overload.

The Shape of Waiting

Time slows down; each second drags,
Hearts in silence, hope still lags.
Watchful eyes on the distant line,
Anticipation, a heavy sign.

Shadows stretch as daylight wanes,
Courage weathers, while patience gains.
In stillness, we weave our fate,
With every breath, we contemplate.

Glimpses of the Invisible

In the folds of silent night,
Unseen worlds dance just from sight.
Whispers gather in the dark,
Fleeting visions leave their mark.

A flicker here, a shimmer there,
Tales untold linger in air.
Between the lines, lay secrets vast,
The past entwined with shadows cast.

Thresholds of Potential

At dawn's embrace, shadows unfold,
Dreams take shape, ambitions bold.
Each step forward, a choice to make,
The paths before us, ours to stake.

The air is thick with futures bright,
Within each heart lies hidden light.
So step with courage, take a chance,
For life awaits in every dance.

Fragments of Future Foundations

Scattered pieces on the floor,
Each a glimpse of what's in store.
Hopeful whispers weave through time,
In every scrap, a chance to climb.

Beneath the rubble, vision thrives,
Old dreams linger, yet new ones rise.
With every fragment, stories grow,
A rich tapestry, yet to show.

The Sigh of Silent Structures

In quiet halls where echoes dwell,
The walls recount their tales to tell.
With every crack, a secret sigh,
The weight of history drifting by.

Forgotten forms in twilight's glow,
The past persists, yet moves so slow.
Among still shadows, memories dance,
Capturing moments, lost in trance.

Faded Lines on a Planner's Canvas

On pages worn, intentions fade,
But dreams continue, undismayed.
Each line once bold, now ghostly traced,
In silent hopes, our time embraced.

Beneath the surface, plans are spun,
In whispered thoughts, the battles won.
Even as colors start to wane,
The spirit of vision will remain.

Pathways to an Infinite Maybe

Whispers of life call softly,
Through fields of endless wonder.
We dance on the edge of fate,
Chasing what lies yonder.

Each step leads to a new twist,
Where horizons blur and blend.
Possibilities beckon bright,
On journeys without end.

Fleeting dreams ride the breeze,
In laughter and silent sighs.
Traveling paths uncharted,
Under wide, watchful skies.

Hope glimmers in the dusk,
Lighting corners of our hearts.
We hold on to our maybe,
Each choice—a work of art.

Unraveled Concepts in the Concrete

Grey towers loom above us,
Veils of stone and steel unite.
Yet thoughts drift beneath the din,
In shadows void of light.

Fragments of dreams lay scattered,
Like leaves upon a street.
Ideas breaking like the dawn,
Awakening the beat.

Each corner hides a secret,
A truth waiting to unfurl.
In the cracks of human hustle,
Lie the answers to our world.

We weave our minds together,
In this dance of heart and art.
Through the rubble and the ruins,
We find a brand new start.

Blueprints of Illusion

Sketches line the faded walls,
Drawn by hands unseen.
In a world of shifting lines,
Nothing is quite as it seems.

Buildings sway with whispered tales,
Mirages in the night.
We chase the dreams we build,
In flickers of false light.

Plans drawn in the outer air,
Flicker like a flame.
We chase the phantoms of our hope,
But they never stay the same.

Yet beneath the shifting ground,
Everything finds its place.
In this web of sweet illusion,
We find our saving grace.

Shadows of an Unfinished Dream

In the corners of my mind,
Echoes of what could be.
Dreams hang like morning fog,
Veiling all I see.

Each moment holds a promise,
Of stories yet untold.
In shadows deep and silent,
A world waits to unfold.

Fragments of a longing heart,
Dance upon the breeze.
In twilight's soft embrace,
We search for sweet release.

Though the path is long and winding,
With choices left to make.
We wander through the shadows,
In hope of light to wake.

The Scaffolded Heart

Within the frame of tender ties,
A heartbeat echoes in the skies.
Built with hope, each layer tight,
An art of love in gentle light.

Worn by scars that tell the tale,
Of storms endured and whispers pale.
Yet strong it stands, though worn and frail,
A fortress grand where dreams prevail.

Every board, a story spun,
Moments lost and battles won.
A structure vast where passions grow,
In every creak, the heart will show.

So let the world, with all its noise,
See the scaffold, hear the joys.
For in this heart, both wild and free,
Love builds a home, eternally.

Fragments of a Journey

Scattered pieces on the ground,
Whispers of dreams that once were found.
Every step, a tale untold,
In the silence, the memories unfold.

Through winding paths and starlit nights,
Chasing shadows, seeking lights.
Each fragment holds a hidden spark,
Guiding souls through the endless dark.

Moments slip like grains of sand,
In shaky grasp, we understand.
Embracing all that life bestows,
From every end, a new start grows.

With every choice, the map we draw,
The heart, it swells, the spirit raw.
In fragments, we find our way,
A journey lived, come what may.

Between the Lines of Creation

In the stillness, whispers dwell,
Of stories bound, the heart's own spell.
Between the lines where dreams collide,
Imagination's force, our guide.

Brushstrokes dance on canvas white,
Colors clash, igniting light.
Voices echo in the air,
In every silence, journeys stare.

Chasing visions, wild and free,
Crafting worlds for all to see.
In the spaces, magic brews,
Between the lines, our truths renew.

So let us write, let us paint,
Create a realm where hearts can faint.
For in these lines, our souls align,
Between the chaos, we find the divine.

The Weight of Unmade Dreams

Heavy lies the heart's desire,
Unmade dreams that burn like fire.
In shadows deep, they bide their time,
Whispers lost in silent rhyme.

Each wish unspooled like tangled thread,
Throughout the night, the longing fed.
A weight that pulls, a cosmic force,
Guiding souls back to their source.

What could have been, a haunting thought,
In the silence, battles fought.
Yet in the ache, a lesson gleams,
From ashes rise unyielding dreams.

So let us chart our course anew,
Tread softly, for what's inside is true.
Though dreams may wait, they never die,
Their whispers echo, reach for the sky.

Point of View from the Edge

I stand upon the weathered stone,
Gazing at the world unknown.
The winds of change around me play,
Whispers of dawn and dusk's decay.

Horizons stretch like tales untold,
In colors rich, and shadows bold.
A silent scream, a heart's lament,
Balancing dreams, so heaven-sent.

Life's slipping threads weave in and out,
Fragile as the fleeting doubt.
Yet here I cling, on this thin line,
To seek the truths that brightly shine.

The edge is sharp, yet clear my sight,
Boundless horizons in the night.
With every breath, I learn to see,
The beauty of this vast decree.

The Ghosts of Once-Intended Endeavors

Whispers dance where shadows tread,
Echoing paths where dreams have fled.
Each choice a flicker, lost in time,
A melody of hollow chime.

Forgotten letters fill the air,
Words unsaid that linger there.
In corners dark, they softly sigh,
The hopes that dared to rise and fly.

Faded visions, shapeless forms,
In memory's grasp, the heart still warms.
Regrets entwined, like ivy green,
In haunted halls where they've once been.

Yet in the silence, seeds are sown,
For every loss, a faith has grown.
These ghosts remind, though paths may veer,
Endeavors lost can still bring cheer.

Tresses of Tangled Dreams

In twilight's glow, the colors blend,
A tapestry where hopes ascend.
With every strand softly entwined,
A story waits for hearts to find.

The dreams once scattered by the breeze,
Now woven tight, like autumn leaves.
Each twist and turn, a choice well made,
In the loom of life, we're not afraid.

With tangled threads, the heart does sing,
Of all the joy that weaving brings.
A crown of visions, bold and bright,
Creating paths out of the night.

Set free the whispers, let them roam,
With every braid, we find our home.
In this embrace, forever stay,
Tresses of dreams, lead the way.

Halfway to Eternity

Beneath the stars, a journey lies,
In moonlit paths, where time complies.
Halfway between the night and dawn,
A fragile hope, forever drawn.

Each step reveals a hidden song,
In echoes soft where hearts belong.
With every heartbeat, we align,
In this dance of fate, divine.

The horizon glows, a tender hue,
As shadows fade and dreams come true.
With open arms, we greet the morn,
In this transition, new souls are born.

Halfway we tread, yet never lost,
In love and light, we pay the cost.
This moment holds, so dear, so free,
Embrace the path to eternity.

The Delicate Balance of Yearning

In silence, whispers softly weave,
A longing heart, unable to leave.
Stars twinkle, secrets in the night,
Caught between shadows and the light.

Waves crashing on an endless shore,
Each ripple sings what we adore.
Fingers trace paths unmeant to cross,
In dreams, we find both gain and loss.

Yearning drips like morning dew,
Tender moments, fragile and true.
With every hope, a weight we bear,
A dance of joy and deep despair.

Yet in this space, sweet ache resides,
Where love and longing softly bide.
The heart knows what the mind can't say,
In quiet corners, it finds a way.

Edifices of What If

What if dreams were built in stone?
Each choice a layer, brightly shone.
Beyond the clouds, we dare to tread,
In shadows cast by words unsaid.

What if laughter filled the halls?
Echoes dancing off these walls.
Moments stacked like bricks so high,
Reaching out to touch the sky.

What if hopes were never lost?
Would we count the endless cost?
Every wish a spire, raised,
In this structure, unamazed.

What if love were time's embrace?
A fortress built in sacred space.
In every heart, a blueprint's drawn,
The past and future, forever on.

Contours of Desire

Soft shadows curve like gentle sighs,
Mapping dreams beneath the skies.
Fingers dance on skin so warm,
Tracing paths in every form.

Whispers float on evening air,
Promises linger, sweet and rare.
In every glance, a story told,
In silent moments, passions bold.

Desire's flame, it flickers bright,
Chasing darkness, yielding light.
In every heartbeat, shadows play,
Contours shifting, night and day.

With every breath, we come alive,
In this rhythm, we survive.
The world dissolves, just you and me,
In the contours of what could be.

Haphazard Skylines

Skyscrapers jut, a crooked line,
Defying angles, dreams intertwine.
Concrete giants scrape the blue,
In every crack, hearts break through.

Windows flash with hidden tales,
Every story wins and fails.
Amidst the chaos, beauty grows,
In the haphazard, life bestows.

Clouds drift lazily past the peaks,
Where silence falls and the heart speaks.
In the clamor, find the grace,
In every corner, a sacred place.

Night descends, the city breathes,
A tapestry of hopes and wreaths.
In scattered lights, our dreams align,
Woven tightly in a haphazard shine.

Unraveled Necessities

In the silence of the night,
Whispers weave through the air,
Needles stitch the frayed seams,
Hopes tangled everywhere.

Beneath the weight of dreams,
Fragile threads collide and break,
Yet new patterns emerge,
From every chance we take.

In the dance of lost desires,
We find the strength to breathe,
Each unraveling moment,
A gift that we receive.

Embracing what we lack,
We gather every piece,
Crafting from the shadows,
A tapestry of peace.

In the Void of Promise

In shadows where the echoes play,
Promises drift like leaves,
Carried on a fleeting wind,
Whispered by forgotten eves.

Each moment holds a secret,
A heartache yet to bloom,
In the void of hope's embrace,
We linger in the gloom.

Stars blink against the dark,
A silent hymn of chance,
Lighting up the path ahead,
Inviting us to dance.

With every step, we falter,
Yet courage finds a way,
In the void of promises,
We seek the light of day.

Contrasts of the Undone

In shadows deep with light that dims,
Life unfolds in whispers thin,
Contrasting dreams with broken seams,
We search for what might have been.

The tapestry of dusk unfurls,
Patterns shift with every breath,
Fragile threads of muted pearls,
Illustrate the hands of death.

Yet in the space where hopes reside,
Resilience carves its place,
Through the messy shades of gray,
We find a truer grace.

Amidst the tales of what we lack,
Echoes of the past will stay,
In the contrasts we embrace,
We forge a brighter way.

Half-Lit Avenues

Through half-lit avenues we roam,
With dreams that flicker low,
Each street a path to somewhere new,
In the shadows, whispers flow.

Grains of sand beneath our feet,
Time slips through our hands,
In every corner lies a spark,
A chance to take new stands.

The moonlight casts its silver hue,
Guiding hearts that seek,
With every step, the world unfolds,
The brave find strength unique.

In half-lit avenues we learn,
To trust the night's embrace,
For even in the dimmest light,
There's hope for every trace.

The Palette of Ambiguity

Colors blend, a hazy hue,
Shades of doubt, what's false, what's true?
A brushstroke here, a smudge, a line,
In every choice, a twist divined.

Whispers in gray, they softly mingle,
Between the notes, where truths can tingle.
The canvas waits, with secrets to bear,
Inviting eyes, to see, to dare.

Patterns shift in the light of day,
Unraveling thoughts in subtle play.
A masterpiece, yet incomplete,
In each confusion, possibilities meet.

With every splash, emotions surge,
In uncertainty, we feel the urge.
To paint a world where meanings sway,
A dance of light, our chosen way.

Jumbled Perspectives

A mirror reflects a fractured scene,
Truths collide, what could have been.
Angles twist, and thoughts entwine,
In the chaos, a clearer sign.

Voices echo in fragmented tones,
Carving paths through shadowy zones.
Perceptions shift like sands of time,
Each viewpoint a puzzle, a silent rhyme.

What seems right may not be clear,
In every glance, a distant sphere.
Connecting dots, we seek the whole,
In the jumbled pieces, we find our soul.

A tapestry woven in shades of thought,
Threads of ideas that luck has brought.
Together they form a story raw,
Woven from life, a vibrant law.

Timelines of Potential

Paths diverge at every turn,
In possibilities, we brightly burn.
Moments stretch, like elastic dreams,
A future waiting in fragile seams.

Choices ripple in the fabric wide,
Augmented realities, worlds collide.
With each decision, a new road grows,
In the garden of time, potential flows.

The clock ticks on, yet stands still here,
In echoes of what we hold dear.
Thread by thread, we weave our place,
In timelines endless, we seek our grace.

Every heartbeat, a chance to choose,
Contemplating the paths we could lose.
In the labyrinth of time, we roam,
Crafting futures, we create our home.

Skirting the Edge of Existence

On the brink, where shadows play,
Life whispers soft, then fades away.
In fleeting moments, we stand amazed,
At the fragile lines that we have grazed.

The edge beckons, a silent call,
Reminding us of the rise and fall.
Every heartbeat teeters on chance,
In the dance of fate, we find our stance.

Between the known and the unexplored,
Lies the essence of dreams we've stored.
With every breath, we push the veil,
Navigating through storms that wail.

A delicate balance of joy and fear,
In edges blurred, we draw near.
To exist is to wade through the fray,
In the brink of life, we learn to sway.

The Walls That Never Were

In shadows built on whispered dreams,
A fortress formed from silent screams.
They rise and fall with fleeting grace,
Yet never hold a true embrace.

A canvas cloaked in starlit night,
Where hopes and fears blend out of sight.
These barriers forged in empty air,
Reflect the wishes we all share.

In echo's grasp they softly sway,
Defining lines that fade away.
They bind us close, then drift apart,
These walls that never held the heart.

Archways to the Unattained

Beneath the arches, dreams abound,
Each step leads to untrodden ground.
Golden light spills through the cracks,
A beckoning call that never lacks.

Paths intertwine in whispered grace,
Carving stories in time and space.
Each turn a choice, a soft refrain,
Through archways echoing joy and pain.

Yet still, they stand, a solemn stare,
Through gates unseen, we search the air.
For every sight we wish to claim,
Archways call us, yet none the same.

Structures of the Unseen Vision

Cascading thoughts in endless flow,
Designs emerge from depths we know.
Structures built on dreams undone,
With every fear, a battles won.

In corners dark, ideas bloom,
Carved in silence, dispelling gloom.
Imagined forms that twist and swell,
In every heart, a secret spell.

These visions roam through veils of time,
A constant pulse, a silent rhyme.
In the unseen, we find our way,
To structures lost, yet here they stay.

Fractured Designs in Time

Time weaves tales in fractured threads,
A tapestry where joy misled.
Each segment speaks of moments passed,
In designs strange, too vast to grasp.

Broken echoes of laughter swell,
In fragmented paths where shadows dwell.
Lines upon lines, a jumbled state,
Creating chaos we contemplate.

But in each cut, there's beauty found,
A universe in whispers bound.
These fractured forms tell stories bright,
In jagged edges, sparks ignite.

Design in Limbo

Patterns dance in twilight glow,
Hopes and fears in ebb and flow.
Sketches hang on silent walls,
Waiting for a voice that calls.

Colors bleed in soft disguise,
Whispers drown beneath the skies.
Formless dreams in corners fold,
Stories left unpenned, untold.

Each intention stretched like wire,
Caught between the tamed and dire.
Fleeting visions haunt the night,
Bound by shadows, lost from sight.

In the balance hangs creation,
Sculpted doubt fueled by frustration.
Yet through chaos, light will seep,
Awakening what lies asleep.

The Unfinished Narrative

Ink trails blur upon the page,
Words collide and disengage.
Stories wander, paused mid-flight,
Leaving echoes in the night.

Characters drift in silent grace,
Lost in time, they leave no trace.
Fragments whisper in the dark,
Fragments spark a hidden arc.

Plotlines twist without a guide,
Yearning for somewhere to abide.
Unraveled plots in tangled seams,
Scattered across unfinished dreams.

Yet perhaps in these disarrayed lines,
Truth of life softly aligns.
In the gaps, new tales may grow,
In the pause, the heart will know.

Skeletal Dreams

In the dark, shadows linger,
Fingers trace their ghostly finger.
What was whole now wears so thin,
Frayed illusions lie within.

Structures lean, drawn toward the void,
Lost ambitions, dreams destroyed.
Hollow echoes fill the air,
Faintly whispering of despair.

A dance of bones in moonlit night,
Chasing phantoms, seeking light.
Breath of life hangs in the chill,
A fragile promise, a lost thrill.

Yet within this skeletal form,
Lies the ember, hope is born.
From the ruins, new seeds will bloom,
Life finds a way beyond the gloom.

Fraying Edges of Tomorrow

Threads unravel, futures fray,
Caught in whispers of decay.
Promises made, now torn apart,
Dreams once bright, now pale and smart.

Moments flicker, fade like mist,
Nothing held in iron fist.
Time's cruel hands, they gently pull,
Whisper soft, their touch can lull.

Hope clings to frayed seams,
Holding fast to fractured dreams.
In the gaps, a spark ignites,
Guiding souls through endless nights.

Though edges fray and world may bend,
Threads of fate will still extend.
In the weave, a tapestry,
Of all the things we dare to be.

Visions Lost in Translation

Whispers drift on distant shores,
Unspoken words through open doors.
Meaning fades like mist at dawn,
In the silence, hope is gone.

Fragments of a tale once told,
Shattered dreams beneath the mold.
Each sigh echoes in the night,
As shadows dance without a light.

Lost in thoughts that twist and turn,
Yearning hearts that ache and burn.
Promises carved in fleeting sand,
Slip through the fingers of a hand.

Glimmers of what might have been,
Traces left, but rarely seen.
In the gap where truth resides,
Answers hide where doubt abides.

Map of the Not Yet

Drawn in dreams on parchment skies,
A journey waits beneath our eyes.
Paths unwoven, yet to tread,
Signs of hope in words unsaid.

Mountains rise, valleys fall,
Landscapes change when duty calls.
Stars align in cosmic threads,
Mapping out the life we shed.

Uncharted realms of what could be,
Every step a mystery.
Footprints linger in the sand,
Leading us to futures planned.

With every breath, we find the way,
Tracing paths through night and day.
In the silence, visions bloom,
Filling voids, dispelling gloom.

Traces of a Forgotten Blueprint

Ink-stained pages, torn and frayed,
Echoes of a dream delayed.
Blueprints sketched with fragile hands,
Outline of forgotten lands.

Worn reflections in cracked glass,
Moments lost, like wisps of grass.
Patterns weave through time and space,
Fragmented joy, a wistful trace.

Every corner holds a sigh,
Stories linger, passing by.
In the shadows, whispers call,
Carving paths, revealing all.

Hidden truths within the lines,
Blueprints drawn by ancient signs.
With each heartache, lessons taught,
In the silence, solace sought.

Where Light Meets the Imperfect

In the cracks where shadows play,
Light emerges, brightening gray.
Imperfections tell our tale,
Each flaw adds to the detail.

Rays of hope in fading light,
Comfort found in endless night.
Through the flaws, we learn to see,
Beauty born of humility.

Every scar a story shared,
Wounds that show how much we cared.
Imperfect hearts beat just the same,
Claiming love without the shame.

In the blend of wrong and right,
Lives entwined in endless fight.
Where light falls, shadows retreat,
Together in a dance so sweet.

Dreams Built on Sand

Whispers of hope in the breeze,
Fragile as dunes, they teeter and sway.
A castle of wishes, soon to appease,
Yet tides of reality wash them away.

Footprints fade near the horizon's glow,
Promises linger, like shadows that wane.
Each grain a story, a tale of woe,
Yet still we build, again and again.

With every sunset, the sky displays,
Colors of dreams that dance and expand.
But morning reveals in its cruel ways,
The truth beneath dreams built on sand.

So we'll chase the light, though it may get blurred,
Fingers entwined in the twilight's embrace.
For in every crumb, there's a heart stirred,
A wish, a hope, a fleeting trace.

The Null Spaces

Between the lines, the silence flows,
A void where thoughts seek to collide.
In empty chambers, a question grows,
What lies beyond when feelings subside?

Echoes fall in the vast unknown,
Where shadows of dreams have come to rest.
In vacant rooms, we're all alone,
Searching for solace, a hidden quest.

The whispers linger, yet fade away,
Under the weight of unspoken lines.
In this silence, we quietly stay,
Caught in the web of our own designs.

Are we the echoes that never depart?
Or fleeting moments, mere flickers of time?
In these null spaces, we question the heart,
Longing for meaning, elusive and prime.

Tenuous Connections

Threads of memory weaving through,
A tapestry fragile, each moment a care.
We grasp at the fleeting, each fondness true,
Yet know in our hearts, they're never quite there.

With laughter that shines like a glimmer of hope,
And eyes that reflect unspoken despair.
We stretch and we reach, learn again how to cope,
But distance remains, an invisible snare.

Every handshake a dance, every smile a bridge,
Yet storms of confusion can tear them apart.
In shadows we wander, on the edge of the ridge,
Holding our breath, with a hopeful heart.

For we are all searching, for moments unique,
In tenuous ties, we find grace in the fall.
Though fleeting the bonds and sometimes oblique,
In their subtle beauty, we answer the call.

Foundations of Maybe

Brick by brick, we ponder the cause,
What lies beneath these dreams we mold?
In shadows of doubt, we build with pause,
Foundations of maybe, both timid and bold.

Mirages of futures dance in the air,
With whispers of fortune, both glitter and dust.
We dream of the heights, yet temper the dare,
In hope and in caution, entwined like a must.

What if tomorrow, the sky should fall?
What if the promises fade in the night?
Still we construct, though we fear it all,
Building a world where our hearts take flight.

So lay down your visions, though shaky they seem,
For in every maybe, a chance to embrace.
Together we nurture the fragile, the dream,
With foundations of maybe, we find our place.

Whispers of Abandonment

In the silence, shadows creep,
Where memories lie, lost in sleep.
Echoes murmur through the night,
Fading hearts and dimming light.

Forgotten dreams, cast aside,
A haunting chill that will not hide.
In empty halls, the walls lament,
A tale of love that time has bent.

Glimmers fade in the soft mist,
Of moments shared that we still missed.
Whispers linger in the air,
Of glimpses once full, now just rare.

Yet in the void, a seed remains,
Of hope that wrestles with the pains.
For in abandonment, we find,
The strength to heal, reclaim our mind.

Fragments of a Vision

Shattered dreams on the cold floor,
Pieces scattered, nothing more.
A glimpse of light behind the dark,
A flicker, still ignites a spark.

Reflections dance on broken glass,
In fleeting moments, we surpass.
Dreams once whole, now torn apart,
Yet in each shard, lies a heart.

Colors merge in a painted sky,
Fragments speak, and they don't lie.
Visions fade, but never die,
In pieces, we learn to fly.

From chaos born, a story we weave,
In every break, the soul can cleave.
Through fragments, we find our way,
To a brighter, bolder day.

Structures of the Unseen

Within the lines of shadowed walls,
Lies a world that gently calls.
Whispers built on fleeting dreams,
Structures formed from silent themes.

Layers deep, we cannot trace,
The hidden paths that leaves no place.
In the quiet, truth unfolds,
A map of hearts that time beholds.

Frameworks sway, yet do not break,
In unseen strength, we start to wake.
Foundations laid in courage's stance,
Chasing shadows in a dance.

We build with faith, though unseen hands,
The architectures of our plans.
In every crack, a story sings,
Structures strong, with hidden wings.

Incomplete Silhouettes

Figures blur in twilight's gaze,
Incomplete in a fading haze.
Shadows linger, half revealed,
In the quiet, truths concealed.

Edges frayed, yet still we stand,
Carved by time, a gentle hand.
In whispers low, the past resides,
The silhouettes of love that hides.

Fragments of us, a work of art,
Incomplete, yet, we won't part.
Each missing line holds a story,
In shadows cast, we find our glory.

Breathe in the night, embrace the void,
Incomplete sketches, we find joy.
For in the gaps, our spirits soar,
Incomplete silhouettes, forever more.

The Remnants of Aspirations

Whispers of hopes lie still,
Faded echoes in the room.
Once they danced on dreams' bright hill,
Now they weave through shadows' gloom.

Fragments of what could have been,
Scatter like dust in the air.
Each wish held tightly within,
Yet freedom calls with a dare.

Time stands still, yet moves along,
Each tick a reminder stark.
Joy and sorrow now belong,
Together they light the dark.

But in the silence, a flame,
A spark of courage ignites.
Resilience, a fierce name,
Guides through the endless nights.

Spaces Between Breath and Thought

In the stillness, moments freeze,
Suspended just for a breath.
Thoughts linger, like soft breeze,
Carving echoes of life and death.

Between the gaps where dreams reside,
Lies the silence of the mind.
A canvas where hopes can collide,
Painting visions, undefined.

Each heartbeat, a silent song,
Pulsing through the void of time.
In these spaces, we belong,
Finding rhythm in the rhyme.

Every pause is a doorway,
To realms yet unchased, unseen.
In the stillness, we will stay,
Chasing dreams that might have been.

Unwritten Plans in Starlit Silence

Beneath the blanket of the night,
Stars twinkle with whispers bold.
Unwritten plans take to flight,
In stories waiting to unfold.

Across the canvas of the dark,
Dreams are painted in soft hues.
Each glimmered point a tiny spark,
Of futures wrapped in quiet muse.

Silhouettes of hope appear,
In the shadows of the sky.
Each wish a pulse crystal clear,
Beneath the vastness, we sigh.

In this silence, paths arise,
Guiding souls through time's vast sea.
In dreams, our destinies lie,
Crafted gently, we are free.

Dreams on the Drafting Table

Papers scattered, lines in place,
Ideas dance in vibrant hues.
Each concept holds a sacred space,
On this table, life ensues.

Blueprints whisper plans of old,
Sketches mark the paths ahead.
In every stroke, a tale is told,
Of hopes that crave to be fed.

With every draft, the future bends,
In folds of promise, we create.
Vision and will, our trusted friends,
Guiding hands to shape our fate.

The table holds our hearts' design,
Each dream a thread we intertwine.
In this space, our hopes align,
Transforming visions into time.

Beneath the Surface of Intent

Whispers dance in quiet halls,
Echoes of what we conceal.
Intentions buried deep in thrall,
Masking every thought we feel.

Beneath the calm, a storm will brew,
Raging tides of doubt and fear.
Yet in the shadows, beauty grew,
A fragile truth, ever near.

In secret corners, dreams collide,
With visions lost in time's embrace.
We search for hope where fears abide,
Yet find our peace in hidden space.

To grasp the depth of what we seek,
We dive beyond the surface guise.
In waters dark, we learn to speak,
And find the light that never dies.

Structures on the Edge

Brick by brick, we build our dreams,
On foundations frail and worn.
Atop the cliff, the skyline gleams,
Yet whispers warn of storms unborn.

Each window framed with hope and doubt,
Steel beams reach for the endless sky.
Yet in the night, a voice will shout,
Challenging the heights we fly.

Beneath the weight of rising fears,
The cracks appear, the shadows creep.
But through the laughter, through the tears,
We find the strength our hearts can keep.

Structures bending, swaying light,
On the edge, we dare to stand.
In trembling grace, we choose the fight,
To claim the dreams we've gently planned.

The Border of Reality

In twilight's hush, we tread the line,
Between what is and what could be.
A fragile thread, a fabled sign,
Where visions blend with mystery.

Through veils of mist, we glimpse the truth,
In colors bright that fade away.
Childlike wonder, eternal youth,
On borders drawn where shadows play.

Each heartbeat marks the rhythm's sway,
Of worlds that merge and intertwine.
Here dreams can dance, and fears decay,
A universe in every sign.

In moments caught, the past aligns,
Reality shifts like sand beneath.
We wander where the heart defines,
The space between, the dream we sheath.

Shattered Plans

Paper dreams strewn on the floor,
Tattered edges tell our tale.
What once was bright is now unsure,
And hope begins to wane and pale.

Each line we drew now fades away,
As storms of change sweep through the night.
The future's clouded, lost in gray,
Yet still, we search for beams of light.

In shattered moments, we find gold,
Fragments glimmer, speak of grace.
Though dreams are broken, hearts are bold,
We rise again, we still embrace.

With every tear, new paths will form,
Beyond the wreckage, strength remains.
In scattered pieces, hearts grow warm,
Until the dawn reveals our gains.

The Promise of Empty Spaces

In corners where shadows softly play,
Whispers of dreams begin to sway.
The silence holds secrets, pure and bright,
In the promise of dawn's gentle light.

Unwritten stories in the air,
Each heartbeat sighs, a gentle prayer.
Hope lingers where the silence grows,
In empty spaces, a beauty flows.

What lies beyond the veil of sight,
A world unfurling, taking flight.
Each breath a canvas, vast and wide,
An endless journey, where dreams reside.

Embrace the stillness, let it be,
A dance of thoughts, wild and free.
For in the quiet, life finds grace,
In the promise of empty spaces.

Drawings in Dust

On weathered roads where footprints fade,
Ghosts of travelers, memories made.
Each grain a story left behind,
In drawings of dust, hope intertwined.

Wind whispers tales through the trees,
A canvas of time, a gentle breeze.
With every step, a mark on the ground,
In the silence, lost dreams abound.

Beneath the sun, they shimmer and glow,
The echoes of laughter, a soft undertow.
In fleeting moments, forever kept,
In drawings of dust, love has we've wept.

So look closely, see the art,
In each tiny particle, beats a heart.
For life is a tapestry, worn yet proud,
In drawings of dust, we stand aloud.

Vertical Reflections

In mirrors positioned high and low,
A glimpse of worlds we do not know.
Each angle bends, reveals the truth,
In vertical reflections, the eyes of youth.

An identity lost, yet found anew,
Cascading visions, a vibrant hue.
What do we see in the glass so clear?
Fragments of selves that draw us near.

Echoes of laughter, shadows of pain,
In every layer, the joy and the rain.
A portrait of life, both bright and dim,
In vertical reflections, we begin to swim.

So study the surface, peer deep inside,
Where contradictions and truths collide.
For in this dance of the light and shade,
Vertical reflections, memories made.

The Haze of Possibility

In the misty dawn where dreams reside,
Possibilities linger, wide and untried.
Each breath a promise, untamed and free,
In the haze of possibility, we dare to be.

Winds of change whisper high and low,
Carrying hopes to where they may grow.
In every heartbeat, a chance to embrace,
The beauty that blooms in each soft space.

Shadows of doubt may cloud our way,
Yet through the fog, we find a ray.
With every step, courage aligns,
In the haze of possibility, destiny shines.

So let us wander, let us explore,
For life unfolds, forevermore.
In this embrace, we learn to see,
In the haze of possibility, we are free.

The Balance Between What Is and What Could Be

In the light of day, we stand tall,
Yet shadows whisper, tempting the fall.
Dreams linger softly on the edge of night,
Yearning for wings, to take flight.

Reality tugs at the seams so tight,
While visions dance just out of sight.
Holding on to hope, we forge our way,
Constructing bridges 'twixt night and day.

Choices are echoes, ringing clear,
Each step a melody, of hope and fear.
Balancing on the tightrope, we sway,
Between what is real and what might stay.

With courage as armor, we face the dawn,
Embracing the dreams woven within the yawn.
For in the heart lies the spark of the free,
The balance between what is and could be.

Pillars of Intention and Hope

In the garden of thoughts, we plant our seeds,
With intentions clear, we care for their needs.
Watered with dreams, they rise from the ground,
Pillars of hope, in silence, profound.

Together we build with hands intertwined,
A sanctuary of wishes, thoughtfully aligned.
Each beam a promise, each stone a vow,
Binding the future, in the here and now.

Through storm and sunshine, steadfast we stand,
Crafting a future, hand in hand.
Nurtured with courage, our spirits ignite,
Pillars of intention, shining bright.

And when the night falls and shadows play,
We anchor our hearts where hopes sway.
For in unity lies the strength we need,
To cultivate love, to plant the good seed.

Blueprints of Uncertainty

Upon the canvas of an unknown fate,
We trace our dreams, steadily create.
Blueprints of uncertainty, drawn with care,
Mapping the paths we dare to share.

Each line uncertain, yet boldly sketched,
In the midst of doubt, our fears are etched.
Colors bleed together, merging as one,
Crafting a journey, where hope has begun.

Each choice a puzzle, shaped with intent,
Yet in disarray, the energies blend.
Through trial and error, we sketch and erase,
Finding our rhythm, setting the pace.

So let us embrace what we cannot see,
With courage and laughter, and hearts wild and free.
For blueprints are merely foundations to lay,
Transforming the chaos, come what may.

Beneath the Surface of Shadows

In the twilight's grip, shadows conspire,
Hiding whispers of dreams that aspire.
Beneath their weight, we find secret streams,
Flowing with truths, with unspoken dreams.

The night holds stories, masked in disguise,
As the heart seeks light, drawn to the skies.
Yet, in the depths where silence is sound,
The essence of hope, in darkness, is found.

Each shadow a lesson, a cloak to unfold,
Bearing the essence of what we've been told.
In the stillness, we gather the night,
To weave through our fears and emerge in the light.

So let us unearth the treasures that lie,
Beneath the surface, where secrets never die.
For in the shadows, with courage unmasked,
We shape our tomorrows, no longer unasked.

Echoes of Uncertainty

In shadows deep, we tread lightly,
Whispers of doubt linger, sprightly.
Paths diverge, choices unfold,
Truths may shimmer, yet feel cold.

Questions swarm like restless bees,
Time slips by with hesitant ease.
Dreams collide in twilight's maze,
Life's a puzzle, a fleeting gaze.

Silence echoes in empty halls,
Fears entwined in fictive walls.
Hope flickers like a candle's flame,
Yet in the dark, we feel the same.

Yet through the doubt, a spark ignites,
Guiding hearts on sleepless nights.
With every fear, a chance to grow,
In uncertainty, we learn to flow.

Foundations in the Fog

Mist shrouds the ground we walk upon,
A world concealed, a silent dawn.
Each step feels like a leap of faith,
Built on dreams, an echo's wraith.

Voices murmur through the haze,
Casting shadows in the blaze.
Foundations shift, we reimagine,
Creating paths with every action.

In fog, the edges softly blur,
Trust the whispers that we confer.
Beyond the veil, a dawn awaits,
Sacred hopes behind hidden gates.

And as the grey begins to lift,
With every heartbeat, we find our gift.
The foundation lies within our hearts,
In fog, the truest journey starts.

The Space Between Plans

In the quiet hours we reside,
Mapping dreams where hopes collide.
Each intention, a thread we weave,
In the spaces, we learn to believe.

Moments pause, like breaths held tight,
Future dances just out of sight.
We draft the sketches of our dreams,
Yet life flows in unexpected streams.

Each plan, a star, bright yet far,
Guides our journey like a distant spar.
In silence, the heart starts to chart,
The unspoken wishes of our heart.

In the space where plans dissolve,
New horizons gently evolve.
And here in the stillness, we expand,
Embracing the shimmer of no man's land.

Half-Built Reveries

Brick by brick, we start to dream,
Chasing shadows, lost in stream.
Half-built towers reach for the sky,
Whispers of what might pass us by.

Fragments of ideas scattered wide,
In the gaps, our passions collide.
A canvas blank yet full of light,
Painted visions, out of sight.

In every flaw, a story waits,
Echoes dancing through silent gates.
The unfinished holds a certain grace,
A glimpse of time and a sacred space.

So let us linger in the grace,
Of half-built dreams in a quiet place.
For every longing that sparks and sways,
Becomes a part of our endless ways.

Dreams Framed in Air

In the quiet of the night, they soar,
Whispers of hope, forevermore.
Framed within the stars' embrace,
Sweet visions drift, a timeless space.

Breath of dawn on fragile seams,
Woven threads of fragile dreams.
A tapestry of wishes bright,
Floating gently into the light.

Lost in the clouds of fleeting time,
Melodies hum, eternally rhyme.
With each heartbeat, new dreams arise,
Painted soft in endless skies.

Ode to the wishes that softly glide,
In realms where hopes and thoughts reside.
Caught in the dance of twilight's glow,
Where dreams in air eternally flow.

Shadows of a Half-Built Haven

In the corners where silence waits,
Shadows linger, weaving fates.
Half-built walls of hopes untold,
Echo softly, brave yet bold.

Windows whisper stories missed,
Fragments of a twilight tryst.
Echoes swirl in the empty hall,
Photographs of none at all.

The light breaks through, yet shadows stay,
In every crevice, dreams at play.
A haven lost in time's cruel grasp,
Lingering futures, forever clasped.

Cracked foundations, tender grace,
In the shadows, we find our place.
A half-built world, a sacred space,
Where hope and heart still interlace.

Foundations of a Faded Fantasy

Beneath the weight of a forgotten dream,
Lie the remnants of once-bright schemes.
Crumbled bricks tell a tale of old,
Of visions that shimmered, now turned to cold.

Faded colors paint the walls,
Resonating with muted calls.
Where laughter lingered, silence reigns,
Dust dances like forgotten trains.

Chasing shadows of distant light,
In whispered echoes, we take flight.
Foundations cracked, yet still they stand,
Hopes interwoven with time's own hand.

In this space of loss and grace,
We search for solace, a warm embrace.
Faded fantasy, yet tender still,
In the ruins, we find our will.

Echoes of Unfinished Spaces

In the echoes of halls unfilled,
Dreams search for voices, long-silenced, stilled.
Timelines stretch in haunting grace,
Boundless realms of a vacant space.

Walls of memory, half-aware,
Crave the heartbeat of dreams laid bare.
Ghosts of laughter dance in air,
Yearning for stories that are not there.

In the creaks of floors and sighs of walls,
We find the beauty in shadowed calls.
Unfinished tales, yet boldly told,
In every crack, new adventures unfold.

Unveiling tales still to define,
In unfinished spaces, we realign.
Holding tight to the dreams we share,
In echoes found, we breathe in air.

Walls of Untold Stories

In shadows deep where whispers lie,
Forgotten tales in silence sigh.
Ghosts of laughter, echoes past,
On crumbling bricks, their shadows cast.

Every crack holds a secret tight,
Dreams woven in the fading light.
Painted memories of joy and pain,
Speak in silence, yet still remain.

Voices call from the stone and dust,
With lives entwined, in love, in trust.
Each layer tells a different fate,
In these walls, we contemplate.

Through windows broken, view the night,
Stars bear witness, gleaming bright.
In the silence, they share their lore,
These walls hold stories forevermore.

The Art of the Unachieved

Brush in hand, a canvas bare,
Dreams and hopes float in the air.
Colors mingle, yet stay unseen,
Life's potential, what might have been.

Plans like sketches lie in wait,
The promise of an open gate.
Brushstrokes falter in mid-flight,
Ideas flicker, dimmed by night.

Lost ambitions, paths untrod,
Hearts once bold, now seem to nod.
What could bloom in vibrant hues,
Is left behind, in silent blues.

Yet in the struggle, beauty thrives,
In every fault, new hope arrives.
The art of dreams that fade away,
Still holds a light, come what may.

Half-Formed Aspirations

Half-formed thoughts like whispered sighs,
Flitter past like fleeting flies.
Fingers stretch to pull them close,
Yet they slip like sand, morose.

In the quiet, doubts convene,
What could grow, remains unseen.
Sketches left upon the page,
Dreams confined, trapped in a cage.

Voices murmur of the chance,
Yearning hearts in a distant dance.
With every try, they start to fade,
In the shadows of plans delayed.

But in that space of wanting more,
Live the hopes that we restore.
Half-formed dreams may still ignite,
A spark of future, waiting bright.

Vistas of What Could Be

Across the hills where shadows play,
Lies a path that guides our way.
In the distance, futures gleam,
Hope and vision, the ultimate dream.

Mountains loom, with peaks so bright,
Calling us to chase the light.
With every step, new worlds unfold,
Stories waiting to be told.

Through valleys rich, the river flows,
Carving paths where possibility grows.
In the breeze, we hear a call,
Echoes of potential, unafraid to fall.

The horizon holds a soft embrace,
Inviting hearts to find their place.
Vistas wide and spirits free,
In the vastness lies what could be.

The Framework of Longing

In shadows deep, where whispers fade,
A heart beats strong, yet feels afraid.
Each thought a thread, a silent plea,
To weave a life, to truly be.

Mountains stand, their peaks on high,
While rivers flow, and time slips by.
Forgotten hopes in twilight's glow,
Stir the depths of longing's flow.

Yet in this pain, a spark ignites,
A flame of dreams, of tranquil nights.
With every step, the path unfolds,
A tapestry of stories told.

And through the storm, the heart remains,
A vessel strong amid the strains.
In longing's grasp, we find our way,
To brighter dawns, a new array.

A World in Suspension

In stillness hangs the morning light,
Time holds its breath, a fleeting sight.
The world at pause, in quiet grace,
Each moment holds a sacred space.

Dreams flutter soft like autumn leaves,
Caught in a web that time deceives.
A symphony, the silence plays,
While hearts prepare for brighter days.

Beneath the hush, potentials grow,
Seeds of purpose, rooted slow.
With every heartbeat, life awaits,
To dance anew, to change our fates.

Suspended now, yet soon we'll soar,
Embracing life, its tales of yore.
A world that waits, with arms held wide,
In precious time, we'll turn the tide.

Nestled Among Aspirations

In gentle folds of whispering dreams,
Nestled among life's vibrant seams.
Ambitions rise like morning sun,
A canvas bright, where hopes are spun.

Each wish a note, in sweet refrain,
A melody within the grain.
With every step, we chase the light,
Together forging paths so bright.

Beliefs like roots, they intertwine,
Strengthening hearts, our spirits shine.
United here, with dreams so bold,
We carve our futures, stories told.

Through valleys deep and mountains high,
A tapestry beneath the sky.
With hands held tight, we face the dawn,
Nestled among what we've drawn.

Rising from the Ashes of Dreams

From shadows cast, where embers reside,
Hope flickers on, a rising tide.
In hushed despair, a spark ignites,
We rise anew, embracing heights.

Through trials faced and battles lost,
Resilience blooms, no matter the cost.
With every breath, we share the fire,
From ashes born, we climb ever higher.

In whispered vows, our spirits mend,
Together we'll journey, hand in hand.
From ruins deep, we build again,
A world reborn, where dreams transcend.

And as the dawn breaks on our soul,
We find our wings, we feel it whole.
Rising strong from dreams once frayed,
In love and hope, our paths are laid.

Echoes Through the Gaps

Whispers dance in silent rooms,
Lost in shadows, lingering gloom.
Each step echoes, soft and frail,
Stories woven, dreams set sail.

Footsteps trace the paths we've made,
In our hearts, where hope won't fade.
Time collects the moments passed,
Echoes hum, a haunting cast.

In between the words we speak,
Lies a truth we rarely seek.
Through the gaps, the silence brews,
Songs of life and shades of blues.

Yet through these echoes, light will bloom,
Filling up the empty room.
A harmony of voices past,
In every heart, their presence cast.

Spaces of the Unwritten

Pages blank, a story waits,
Dreams untold, behind the gates.
In the silence, secrets stir,
Inkless tales that gently blur.

Quiet moments hold their breath,
Yearning words that dance with death.
In the margins, life resides,
Hope and fear, where love abides.

Each heartbeat holds a vacant line,
Futures bright, yet undefined.
In these spaces, shadows loom,
Waiting for the chance to bloom.

Untold journeys lie ahead,
In our minds, where dreams are spread.
These unwritten paths invite,
To wander forth and find the light.

The Fabric of Maybes

Threads of hope, in colors bright,
Woven dreams that catch the light.
In each stitch, a choice awaits,
Fabric rich, our lives create.

Tangled yarns, the doubt we face,
Yet in knots, we find our place.
In the gaps, a story breathes,
In this quilt, our heart believes.

Every fray, a path we trace,
In the chaos, find our grace.
The fabric pulls us, soft and tight,
In the weavings, wrong and right.

With every patch, a tale unfolds,
In the seams, our truth upholds.
Together stitched, we rise above,
In the fabric, we find love.

Incomplete Canvases

Brushes poised on empty ground,
Colors yearn, but silence found.
Every stroke a fleeting thought,
In the canvas, dreams are caught.

Half-formed images take flight,
Whispers dance in shades of light.
In the gaps where colors blend,
Artistry, an endless trend.

Hands that shake, unsure, afraid,
Yet potentials never fade.
In the chaos, beauty brews,
Incomplete, yet still it cues.

Unfinished works, they tell a tale,
Of journeys long, of winds that sail.
In every layer, stories weave,
Incomplete canvases believe.

Milton Keynes UK
Ingram Content Group UK Ltd.
UKHW020044271124
451585UK00012B/1041

9 789916 905654